MW01053605

# SPA DESIGN

daab

# INTRODUCTION

Not too long ago, plain fitness rooms with a plethora of equipment were the epitome of wellness in hotels or studios. That is now a thing of the past. Today, day spas are the "place to be" when it comes to relaxation and regeneration. There are now standards that show where the difference is to a cosmetic salon in the classical sense. The basic components of a good spa are various saunas, a pool, at least two treatment rooms and a relaxation area that offers enough room so that guests do not disturb each other. The new day spa generation emphasizes therapeutic administrations such as, for example, ayurveda, yoga, floating pools or Tibetan singing bowl meditation, for which additional rooms are set up. Almost all newcomers are spread out over an area starting at 300 m², offer places to relax in indoor and outdoor areas and often build a symbiosis with various types of swimming pools and thermal baths. In warmer climates, the spa owners like to offer various treatments outside: massage on a South Sea beach, a facial peeling on the spa terrace of a Spanish resort or meditation courses under Mexican palm trees – anything is possible. The best day spas – in so far as they were not constructed as purely city spas – are components of holistic wellness and relaxation concepts, located in the most beautiful regions on Earth, with spacious guest rooms and suites, excellent cuisine, as well as discriminating design and interiors. A further characteristic of innovative spa complexes is design in the regional style and using customary construction elements – such as Moorish décor from the Middle East. What does the future hold in store? The magic words are "medical wellness" and means medical supervision in the spa centers. In addition to physical treatments, a special emphasis on prevention programs such as check-ups or nutrition consultation will be offered. In this book, "Spa Design", the reader will discover further proof of how multifaceted and individual spas can be.

Vor nicht allzu langer Zeit waren eher schmucklose Fitnessräume mit großem Gerätepark der Inbegriff für Wellness in Hotels oder Studios. Das hat sich grundlegend geändert. Heute sind Day Spas die begehrten „places to be", wenn es um Entspannung, Wohlbefinden und Regeneration geht. Inzwischen gibt es deshalb Standards, die aufzeigen, wo der Unterschied zu einem Kosmetiksalon klassischer Prägung liegt. Zur Grundausstattung eines guten Spas gehören verschiedene Saunen, ein Pool, mindestens zwei Behandlungsräume und ein Ruhebereich, der genügend Platz bietet, damit die Gäste sich nicht gegenseitig stören. Die neue Day Spa-Generation setzt darüber hinaus auf Anwendungen wie zum Beispiel Ayuverda, Yoga, Floatingbecken oder Klangschalen Meditation, für die weitere Räume eingerichtet sind. Fast alle Newcomer breiten sich auf Flächen ab 300 Quadratmetern aus, bieten Orte zum Relaxen im In- und Outdoorbereich und bilden oft eine Symbiose mit Bade- und Thermenlandschaften. In wärmeren Klimazonen verlagern die Betreiber der Spas Behandlungen gerne nach draußen: Massagen am Südseestrand, ein Gesichtspeeling auf der Spa Terrasse eines spanischen Resorts oder Meditations-kurse unter mexikanischen Palmen – alles ist möglich. Die besten Day Spas – sofern sie nicht als reine City Spas errichtet wurden – sind Bestandteile von ganzheitlichen Wellness- und Entspannungskonzepten, in den schönsten Regionen der Erde gelegen, mit großzügigen Gästezimmern und Suiten, einer guten Küche sowie einem hohen Anspruch an Design und Interieur. Ein weiteres Merkmal von innovativen Spa-Anlagen ist die Gestaltung im regionalen Stil und die Verwendung landesüblicher Einrichtungselemente – zum Beispiel im Mittleren Osten maurisches Dekor. Was bringt die Zukunft? Das Zauberwort heißt „Medical Wellness" und steht für eine ärztliche Betreu-ung in den Spa-Centern. Insbesondere Vorsorgeprogramme wie Check-ups oder Ernährungs-beratung werden neben den Körperbehandlungen angeboten. In dem vorliegenden Buch „Spa Design" finden Leser noch viele weitere Belege dafür, wie facettenreich und individuell Spas aussehen können.

Hasta no hace mucho tiempo, el área de relax y salud de los hoteles o los gimnasios consistía en un salón más bien austero con grandes aparatos. Esto ha cambiado radicalmente: hoy en día, los spa se han convertido en "el" lugar donde ir cuando se trata de relajarse, sentirse bien y recuperar energías. Asimismo, ya existen estándares que marcan qué los diferencia de un salón de belleza clásico. El equipamiento básico de un buen spa incluye diferentes tipos de sauna, una piscina, por lo menos dos salas de tratamiento y un área de descanso con suficiente lugar como para que los huéspedes no se molesten entre sí. La nueva generación de spa ofrece también, por ejemplo, yoga, ayurveda o meditación, contando con salas especiales para cada actividad. Casi todos los nuevos centros ocupan superficies de más de 300 metros cuadrados, áreas de relajación interiores y exteriores, y suelen combinarse con propuestas naturales de baños y termas. En las zonas de clima más cálido, los organizadores optan por ofrecer los tratamientos al aire libre: masajes a orillas del océano austral, tratamientos faciales en la terraza de un spa de un resort español o cursos de meditación bajo las palmeras mexicanas. Nada es imposible. Los mejores spa, exceptuando los ubicados en el seno de las ciudades, son parte de conceptos integrales de salud y relajación, están ubicados en las regiones más bellas del planeta, cuentan con amplios cuartos y suites para los huéspedes, ostentan una oferta gastronómica de alto nivel, y son muy exigentes en lo que respecta a la arquitectura y el diseño. Otra característica de los spa innovadores es que se diseñan en armonía con el estilo regional, utilizando elementos típicos del lugar, como, por ejemplo, la decoración mora en el Medio Oriente. ¿Qué nos traerá el futuro? La palabra mágica es "wellness medicinal" y se refiere a la atención médica dentro de un spa. En particular, se ofrecen programas de prevención y control o asesoramiento sobre nutrición, junto con tratamientos. En este libro, "Diseño de Spa", el lector podrá encontrar muchos otros ejemplos de la diversidad e individualidad que logran los spa.

Il y a peu de temps encore, les salles de remise en forme plutôt austères et dotées de nombreux appareils étaient synonymes de wellness dans les hôtels ou les studios. Les choses ont radicalement changé depuis. Aujourd'hui, les „day spas" sont des endroits extrêmement recherchés pour tous ceux qui désirent trouver relaxation, bien-être et régénération. Il existe désormais des standards qui montrent où réside la différence par rapport à un institut de beauté classique. Tout centre spa qui se respecte doit être équipé normalement de divers saunas, d'une piscine, de deux salles de traitement minimum et d'un espace repos offrant suffisamment de place pour que les invités ne se gênent pas mutuellement. La nouvelle génération de „day spas" mise en outre sur des applications complémentaires comme par exemple l'ayuverda, le yoga, les séances de flottement ou la méditation au son de gongs pour lesquelles d'autres salles sont aménagées. Presque tous les nouveaux venus se répartissent sur des surfaces à partir de 300 m2, offrent des espaces de relaxation à l'intérieur et à l'extérieur, formant souvent une symbiose avec les espaces de baignade et le paysage thermal. Dans les zones climatiques plus chaudes, les exploitants de centres spas proposent volontiers des traitements en extérieur : massages sur une plage des mers du sud, gommage facial sur la terrasse d'un spa dans un grand site de villégiature ou cours de méditation sous les palmiers du Mexique. Les meilleurs „day spas" – dans la mesure où il ne s'agit pas de centres spas à vocation purement urbaine – font partie intégrante de concepts globaux de remise en forme et de relaxation situés dans les plus belles régions du monde avec des chambres et des suites spacieuses, une excellente cuisine ainsi que de grandes exigences sur le plan du design et de la décoration intérieure. Une autre caractéristique des centres spa innovateurs est l'aménagement dans le style régional et l'utilisation d'éléments d'ameublement locaux – un décor mauresque au Moyen-Orient par exemple. De quoi sera fait demain ? Le mot magique est „Medical Wellness" avec un encadrement médical dans les centres spa. Des programmes de prévention notamment tels que check-ups ou conseils diététiques par exemple sont proposés en plus des traitements corporels. Dans cet ouvrage intitulé „Spa Design", les lecteurs découvriront encore de nombreuses preuves de la richesse des facettes des centres spas ainsi que de leur individualité.

Non è passato molto tempo da quando lo spazio dedicato al wellness all'interno di alberghi e palestre ancora fu costituito da locali fitness piuttosto spogli, ma con un grande parco macchine. Nel frattempo la situazione è del tutto cambiata. Oggi i cosiddetti day spa sono i più richiesti „places to be" per potersi rilassare, curare il proprio benessere e rigenerarsi. Per questo sono sorti degli standard che fanno vedere le differenze rispetto ad un salone di bellezza classico. Fanno parte dell'attrezzatura elementare di un buono spa diversi tipi di sauna, una piscina, almeno due stanze per i trattamenti e una generosa zona relax in modo che gli ospiti rimangano indisturbati. La nuova generazione di day spa inoltre punta su trattamenti specifici come ad esempio l'ayurveda, lo yoga, la vasca di galleggiamento o la meditazione con campane tibetane, e predispone i relativi locali. Quasi tutti i nuovi arrivati nel settore si estendono su superfici di almeno 300 mq, offrono spazi interni ed esterni per il relax e spesso creano una simbiosi con paesaggi balneari e termali. Nelle zone climatiche più calde, i gestori preferiscono spostare i trattamenti all'esterno: massaggi sulla spiaggia dei Mari del Sud, un peeling facciale sulla terrazza della zona spa di un resort spagnolo oppure corsi di meditazione sotto le palme messicane – tutto è possibile. I migliori day spa – a meno che non siano stati concepiti come city spa – integrano complessivi concetti di wellness e relax e sono situati nelle regioni più belle del mondo, con generose stanze e suites per gli ospiti, una buona cucina ed il design e l'arredamento molto raffinati. L'arredamento nello stile regionale e l'utilizzo di elementi decorativi tradizionali come ad esempio le decorazioni moresche nel Medio Oriente sono altre caratteristiche di impianti spa innovativi. Cosa porta il futuro? La parola magica è il „medical wellness" e sta per l'assistenza medica all'interno dei centri spa. In particolare programmi di prevenzione come il check-up oppure la consulenza dietetica vengono offerti in aggiunta ai trattamenti per il corpo. Nel presente volume „Spa Design" il gentile lettore potrà rendersi conto delle tante sfaccettature individuali dei singoli spa.

**ABRAMSON TEIGER ARCHITECTS | LOS ANGELES**
www.abramsonteiger.com
Dermalogica Spa on Montana
www.dermalogica.com
Los Angeles, CA, USA | 2003
Photos: Lars Frazer

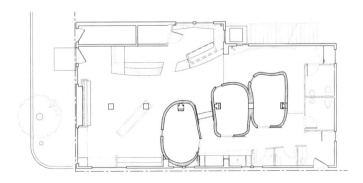

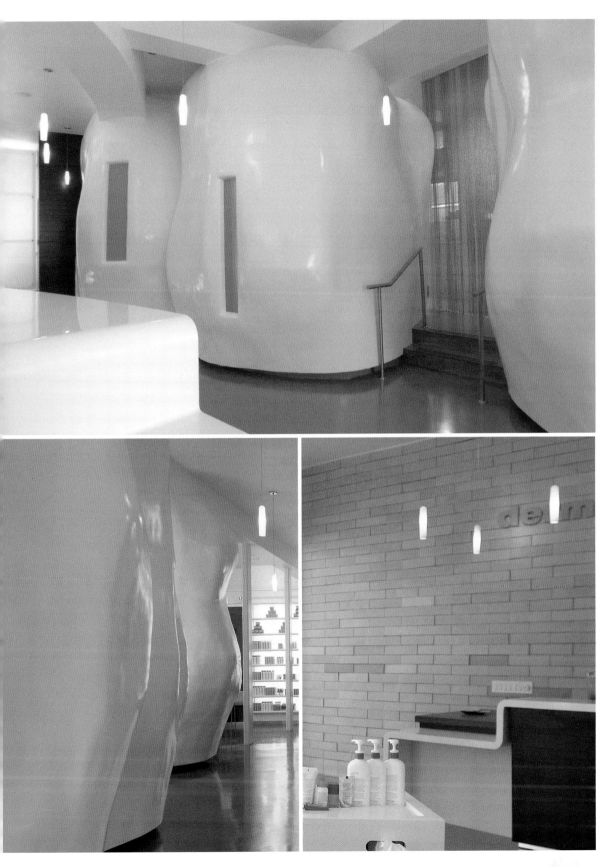

**JONATHAN ADLER** I **NEW YORK**
www.jonathanadler.com
PSYC at The Parker Palm Springs
www.lemeridien.com
Palm Springs, CA, USA I 2005
Photos: Gavin Jackson

**ALDOPLAN AG, VADIAN METTING VAN RIJN**
**IN COLLABORATION WITH VINCENZ ERNI | WEGGIS**
www.aldoplan.ch
Parkhotel Weggis
www.phw.ch
Weggis, Switzerland | 2002
Photos: Fabrik Studios

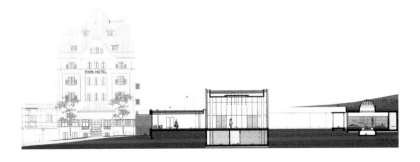

**ALEKS ISTANBULLU ARCHITECTS** | **LOS ANGELES**
www.ai-architects.com
Cerritos County Bathhouse
Cerritos, CA, USA | 2004
Photos: Tom Bonner

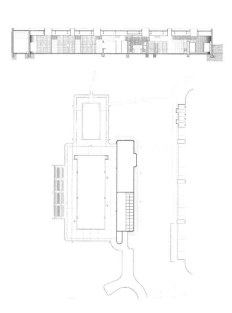

**ALLEN + PHILP ARCHITECTS** I SCOTTSDALE
**JUDY TESTANI WITH TESTANI DESIGN TROUPE (INTERIOR)** I SCOTTSDALE
www.allenphilp.com
Sanctuary on Camelback Mountain
www.sanctuaryoncamelback.com
Paradise Valley, AZ, USA I 2002
Photos: Martin Nicholas Kunz, courtesy Sanctuary on Camelback Mountain

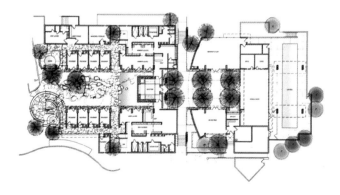

**ANDRÉ BALAZS PROPERTIES | NEW YORK**
**SHAWN HAUSMAN | LOS ANGELES**
www.andrebalazsproperties.com
The Standard Miami
www.standardhotel.com
Miami, FL, USA | 2006
Photos: Martin Nicholas Kunz

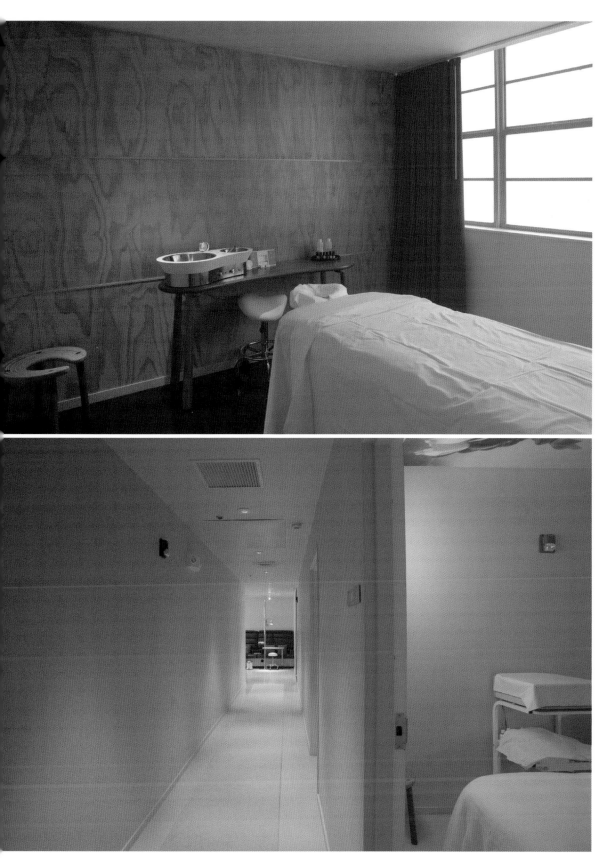

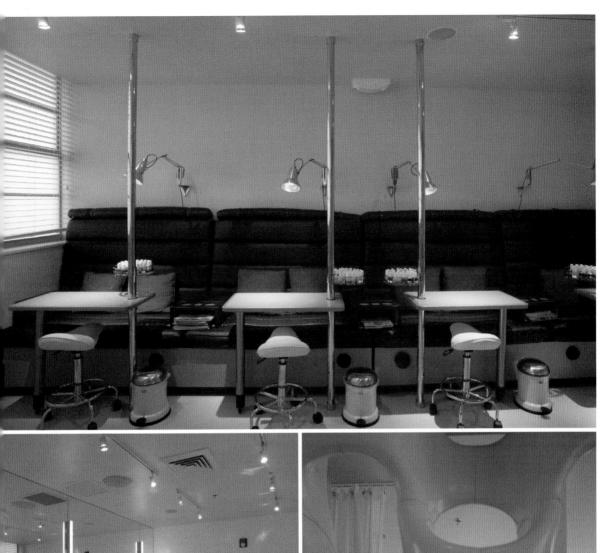

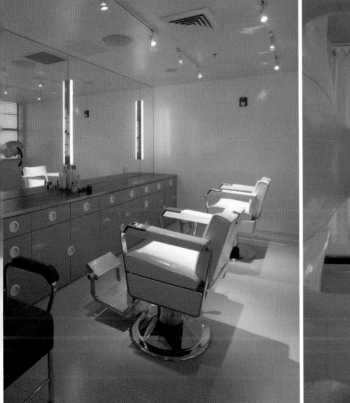

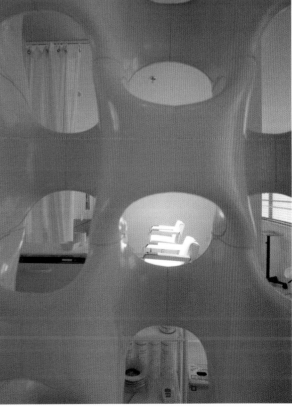

**BEHLES AND PARTNER (ARCHITECTURE) | ZURICH**
**E'SPA | SURREY**
www.ESPAonline.com
E'SPA Victoria Jungfrau
www.victoria-jungfrau.ch
Interlaken, Switzerland | 2003
Photos: Roland Bauer

**BRIAN BRENNAN PROJECTS DIRECTOR BUILDING & DESIGN
FOR RED CARNATION HOTELS I LONDON**
The Sanctuary Spa at the Twelve Apostles Hotel & Spa
www.12apostleshotel.com
Cape Town, South Africa I 2003
Photos: Martin Nicholas Kunz

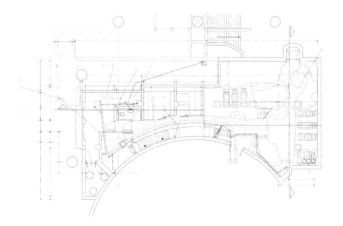

**ALAN CHAN DESIGN, CL3** | **HONG KONG**
www.alanchandesign.com
Evian Spa by Three
www.threeonthebund.com
Shanghai, China | 2004
Photos: courtesy Three on the Bund

**CHHADA, SIEMBIEDA & ASSOC.** | **REDFERN**
www.chhada.com
Ananda Himalaya
www.anandasparesort.com
Uttaranchal, India | 2000
Photos: Martin Nicholas Kunz

**TONY CHI | NEW YORK**
www.tonychi.com
i.sawan at Grand Hyatt Erawan Bangkok
www.bangkok.grand.hyatt.com
Bangkok, Thailand | 2005
Photos: courtesy Hyatt Hotels International

**CREAM | HONG KONG**
www.cream.com.hk
Yoga Plus Spa Center
www.yogaplus.com.hk
Hong Kong, China | 2005
Photos: Virgile Simon Bertrand

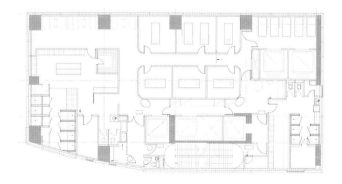

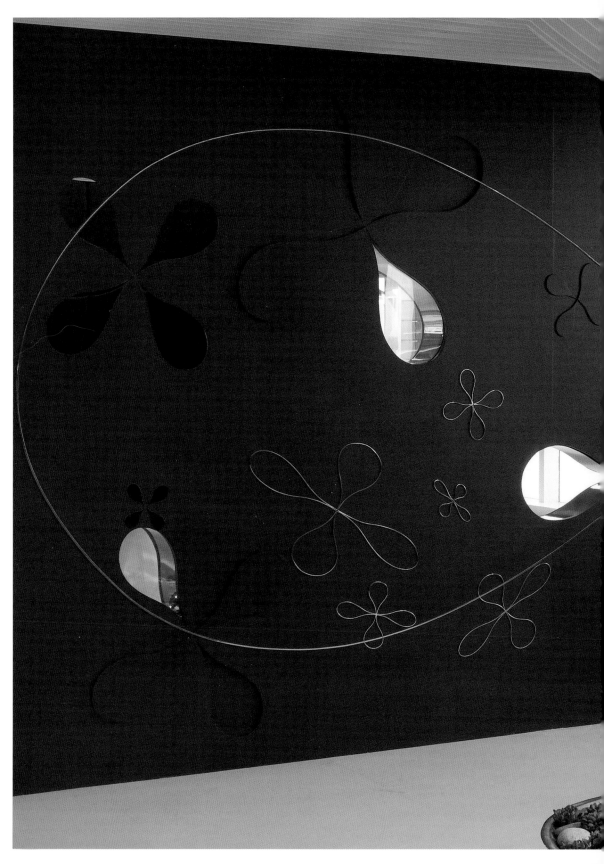

**REGINA DAHMEN-INGENHOVEN** | **DUESSELDORF**
www.ingenhovenundpartner.de
Lanserhof
www.lanserhof.at
Lans, Austria | 2006
Photos: Holger Knauf

**ERICH DAPUNT** I **BOLZANO**
**DR. JOHANNES TONI** I **MERANO**
Unterpazeider
www.unterpazeider.com
Marling, Italy I 2005
Photos: Erich Dapunt, Dr. Karlheinz Sollbauer

**DE MATOS STOREY RYAN** | **LONDON**
www.dmsr.co.uk
Cowley Manor
www.cowleymanor.com
Cowley, United Kingdom | 2002
Photos: David Grandorge

**DAVID EDWARDS OF JAMES PARK ASSOCIATES | SINGAPORE**
**MGIRAUD ARCHITECTS | MAURITIUS**
www.jpadesign.com
Jiva Grande Spa at Taj Exotica Mauritius
www.tajhotels.com
Wolmar, Flic en Flac, Mauritius | 2004
Photos: Martin Nicholas Kunz

**FOBA | KYOTO**
www.fob-web.co.jp
TsukitoHana Spa and Eco Garden
www.tsukitohana.jp
Tokushima, Japan | 2004
Photos: Nacasa & Partners

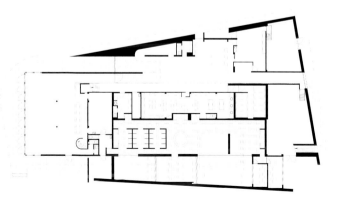

**HANS-PETER FONTANA | FLIMS**
**PIA SCHMID | ZURICH**
www.piaschmid.com
Park Hotel Waldhaus
www.parkhotel-waldhaus.ch
Flims, Switzerland | 2004
Photos: Gaudenz Danuser

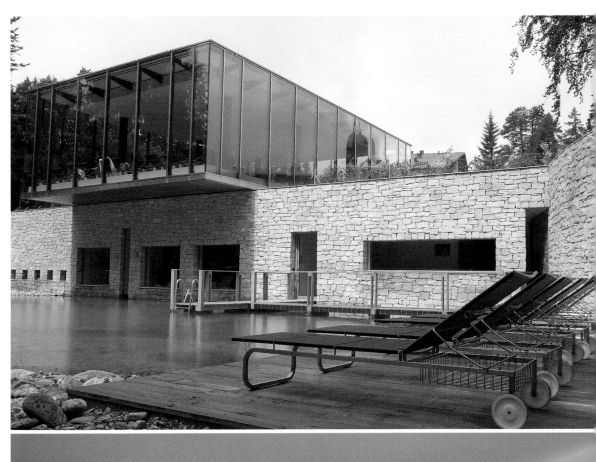

**JACQUES GARCIA (INTERIOR DESIGN) | PARIS**
**PATRICE REYNAUD (ARCHITECTURE) | GENEVA**
www.reynaud.ch
La Réserve Géneva Hotel & Spa
www.lareserve.ch
Geneva, Switzerland | 2003
Photos: Martin Nicholas Kunz, courtesy La Réserve Géneva Hotel & Spa

**JEAN MICHEL GATHY, DENNISTON INTERNATIONAL
ARCHITECTS | KUALA LUMPUR
E'SPA | SURREY**
www.denniston.com.my
www.ESPAonline.com
One&Only Maldives at Reethi Rah
www.oneandonlyresorts.com
Reethi Rah, Maldives | 2005
Photos: courtesy One&Only Resorts

**JEAN MICHEL GATHY (EXTERIOR)** I **KUALA LUMPUR**
**JAYA PRATOMO IBRAHIM OF**
**JAYA & ASSOCIATES (INTERIOR)** I **JAKARTA**
www.denniston.com.my
The Spa at The Setai
www.setai.com
Miami, FL, USA I 2005
Photos: Martin Nicholas Kunz

**PABLO STUTZ OF GIAD UK LIMITED | LONDON**
www.giaduk.com
Hotel Arts Barcelona
www.ritzcarlton.com
Barcelona, Spain | 2005
Photos: courtesy Six Senses Spa / Hotel Arts Ritz Carlton

**GLUCKMAN MAYNER ARCHITECTS** | **NEW YORK**
www.gluckmanmayner.com
Mii amo, a destination spa at Enchantment Resort
www.miiamo.com
Sedona, AZ, USA | 2001
Photos: Martin Nicholas Kunz, courtesy Enchantment Resort

**JOHN HEAH & CO.** | **LONDON**
Four Seasons Bali at Sayan
www.fourseasons.com/sayan
Bali, Indonesia | 2001
Photos: Martin Nicholas Kunz, courtesy Four Seasons Hotels and Resorts

**HIRSCH BEDNER ASSOCIATES (INTERIOR DESIGN)** I **ATLANTA**
**E'SPA** I **SURREY**
**BRENNAN BEER GORMAN (ARCHITECTURE)** I **NEW YORK**
www.hbadesign.com
www.ESPAonline.com
www.bbg-bbgm.com
The Spa at Mandarin Oriental New York
www.mandarinoriental.com/newyork
New York, NY, USA I 2003
Photos: Gavin Jackson, courtesy Mandarin Oriental Hotel Group

**KEITH HOBBS (INTERIOR) | LONDON**
www.united-designers.com
COMO Shambala at Parrot Cay
www.shamnhala.como.bz
Providenciales, Turks and Caicos Islands | 2004
Photos: Francine Fleischer

**KCA INTERNATIONAL, KHUAN CHEW | DUBAI**
www.kca-int.com
Six Senses Spa at Madinat Jumeirah
www.madinatjumeirah.com
Dubai, United Arab Emirates | 2004
Photos: Roland Bauer

**CHRIS KOFITSAS | NEW YORK**
www.nwdbonline.com
tru
www.truspa.com
San Francisco, CA, USA | 2003
Photos: Eric Langel

**KY INTERNATIONAL INC, USA, LEO DESIGNERS PTE LTD
(INTERIOR DESIGN), HUAY ARCHITECTS | SINGAPORE**
Spa Botanica at The Sentosa Resort & Spa
www.thesentosa.com
Singapore, Singapore | 2003
Photos: Martin Nicholas Kunz

**MICHAEL MARQUEZ ARCHITECTS | BRENTWOOD**
www.dynamic.mmarchitectsla.com
Blue Medical Beauty Spa
www.experienceblue.com
Sherman Oaks, CA, USA | 2004
Photos: Ayola Photography

**JOHN MORFORD | HONG KONG**
"Club On The Park" at Park Hyatt Tokyo
www.tokyo.park.hyatt.com
Tokyo, Japan | 1994
Photos: Martin Nicholas Kunz

**JOHN MORFORD** | **HONG KONG**
Plateau
www.plateau.com.hk
Hong Kong, China | 2004
Photos: courtesy Hyatt Hotels International

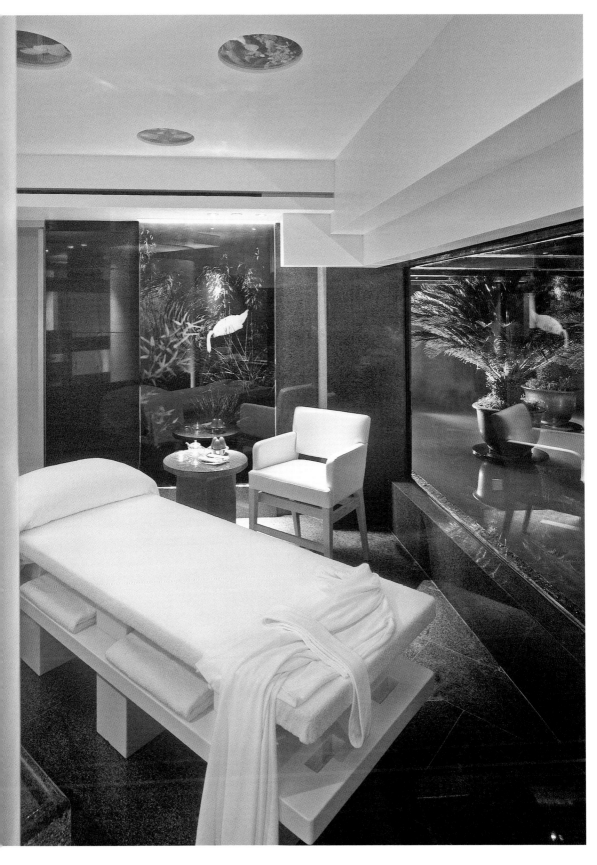

**ATELIERS JEAN NOUVEL | PARIS**
www.jeannouvel.com
Attic at Silken Hotel Puerta America
www.hoteles-silken.com
Madrid, Spain | 2005
Photos: Martin Nicholas Kunz

**P INTERIOR AND ASSOCIATES CO., LTD. (PIA)** I **BANGKOK**
www.pia-group.com
Devarana Spa at Dusit Thani Hotel
www.devaranaspa.com
Bangkok, Thailand I 2001
Photos: courtesy Devarana Spa

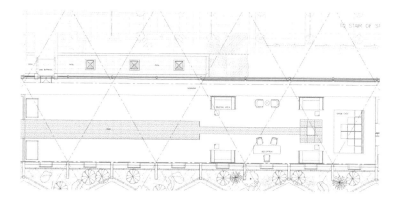

**PAL DESIGN CONSULTANTS LTD, PATRICK LEUNG | HONG KONG**
www.paldesign.cn
Spa MTM
www.mtmskincare.com/spa
Hong Kong, China | 2005
Photos: Steve Mok

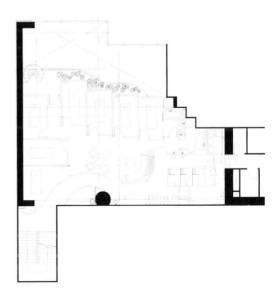

**ANDRÉE PUTMAN** | **PARIS**
www.andreeputman.com
Blue Spa Hotel Bayerischer Hof
www.bayerischerhof.de
Munich, Germany | 2005
Photos: courtesy Hotel Bayerischer Hof

**RAUMFORUM, BALMER UND KRIEG | STEFFISBURG**
www.raumforum.ch
7 sources beauty and spa at Lenkerhof
www.lenkerhof.ch
Lenk, Switzerland | 2002
Photos: Michael Reinhardt

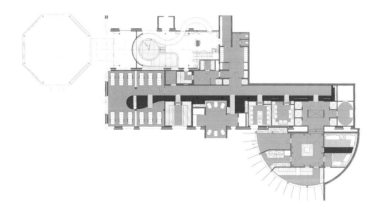

**SILVIO RECH AND LESLIE CARSTENS ARCHITECTURE | JOHANNESBURG**
North Island
www.north-island.com
North Island, Seychelles | 2004
Photos: Dana Allan, Michael Poliza

**ERIC REICHENBACH (INTERIOR DESIGN), GOTTFRIED HAUSWIRTH (ARCHITECTURE) | SAANENMÖSER**
Grandhotel Bellevue Gstaad
www.bellevue-gstaad.ch
Gstaad, Switzerland | 2003
Photos: Roland Bauer

**PETER REMEDIOS (INTERIOR DESIGN), NORBERT
DECKELMANN (ARCHITECTURE) | LONG BEACH**
Oriental Spa at The Landmark
www.mandarinoriental.com
Hong Kong, China | 2005
Photos: courtesy Mandarin Oriental Hotel Group

**EZIO RIVA | MILAN**
E'SPA at Gianfranco Ferré
www.gianfrancoferre.com
Milan, Italy | 2003
Photos: Paola De Pietri

**RICHARDSON SADEKI DESIGN | NEW YORK**
www.richardsonsadeki.com
Bliss 57 New York
www.blissworld.com
New York, NY, USA | 1999
Photos: Richardson Sadeki, Andrew Bordwin Studio, Inc.

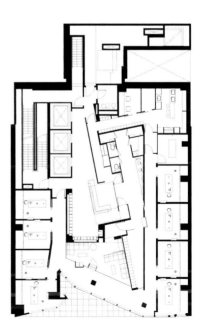

**SEHW ARCHITEKTEN** I **HAMBURG, BERLIN, VIENNA**
www.sehw.de
Holmes Place Hamburg
www.holmesplace.co.uk
Hamburg, Germany I 2003
Photos: Jürgen Schmidt

**SEHW ARCHITEKTEN** I **HAMBURG, BERLIN, VIENNA**
www.sehw.de
Holmes Place Lübeck
www.holmesplace.co.uk
Lübeck, Germany I 2003
Photos: Jürgen Schmidt

**SIX SENSES PROJECT TEAM (BUILDINGS) IN COLLABORATION WITH DWP CITYSPACE LTD. | BANGKOK**
www.sixsenses.com
Earth Spa by Six Senses Spas at Evason Hideaway Hua Hin
www.sixsenses.com/hideaway-huahin
Hua Hin, Thailand | 2005
Photos: courtesy of Six Senses Hotels & Resorts

**GERMAN DEL SOL** | **SANTIAGO DE CHILE**
www.germandelsol.cl
Explora en Atacama
www.explora.com/atacama-e.jsp
San Pedro, Chile | 1998
Photos: Guy Wenborn

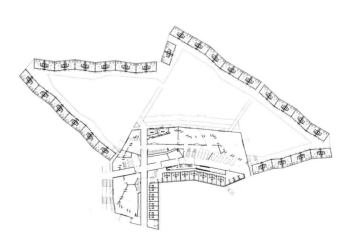

**GERMAN DEL SOL | SANTIAGO DE CHILE**
www.germandelsol.cl
Explora en Patagonia
www.explora.com/patagonia-e.jsp
Patagonia, Chile | 1993
Photos: Guy Wenborn

**GERMAN DEL SOL | SANTIAGO DE CHILE**
www.germandelsol.cl
Spot at the Remota Hotel
www.remota.cl
Puerto Natales, Patagonia, Chile | 2006
Photos: Mcduff Everton, Juan Pablo Gonzalez,
Daniel Gonzalez, Jaime Borquez, Felipe Camus

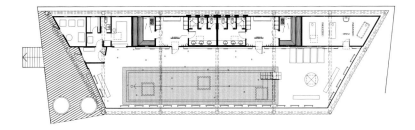

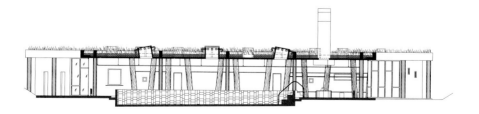

**GERMAN DEL SOL** | **SANTIAGO DE CHILE**
www.germandelsol.cl
Termas Geométricas
www.termasgeometricas.cl
Villarrica, Chile | 2004
Photos: Hanna Martin, Guy Wenborn

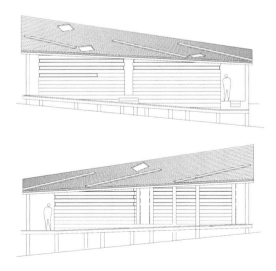

**SWABACK PARTNERS (ARCHITECTURE), HENRIKSEN DESIGN ASSOCIATES (INTERIOR DESIGN) | SCOTTSDALE**
www.swabackpartners.com
Spa Avania at Hyatt Regency Scottsdale
www.spaavania.com
Scottsdale, AZ, USA | 2005
Photos: Martin Nicholas Kunz, courtesy Hyatt Hotels International

**JOSEPH SY & ASSOCIATES** | **HONG KONG**
www.jsahk.com
Zenana
Hong Kong, China | 2005
Photos: Joseph Sy

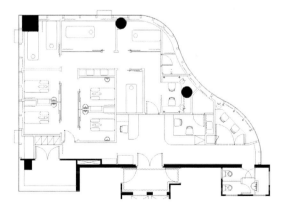

**USHI TAMBORIELLO | MUNICH**
Hamam in Trafo Baden
www.fitnesspark-hamam-baden.ch
Baden, Switzerland | 2005
Photos: Jochen Splett

**THIERRY TEYSSIER** I **PARIS**
Dar Ahlam
www.darahlam.com
Ouarzazate , Morocco I 2002
Photos: Roland Bauer

**EDWARD TUTTLE** I **PARIS**
Amanjena
www.amanjena.com
Marrakech, Morocco I 2000
Photos: Roland Bauer

**VA ARKITEKTAR | REYKJAVIK**
www.vaarkitektar.is
The Blue Lagoon
www.bluelagoon.com
Grindavík, Iceland | 1999
Photos: Ragnar Th. Sigurðsson, Haukur Snorrason

**WILSON AND ASSOCIATES** | **DALLAS**
www.wilsonassoc.com
One&Only Royal Mirage
www.oneandonlyresorts.com
Dubai, United Arab Emirates | 2002
Photos: Martin Nicholas Kunz

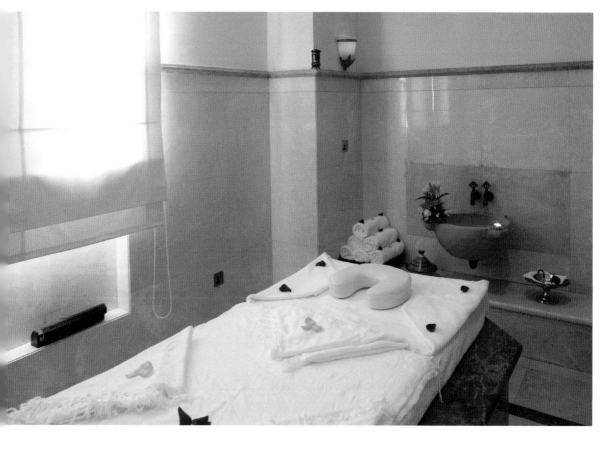

**COLLETT ZARZYCKI | LONDON**
www.collett-zarzycki.com
Sequoia Spa at The Grove
www.thegrove.co.uk
Chandler's Cross, United Kingdom | 2003
Photos: Roland Bauer

**PETER ZUMTHOR | HALDENSTEIN**
Therme Vals
www.therme-vals.ch
Vals, Switzerland | 1996
Photos: Roland Bauer

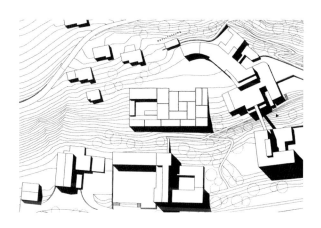

# INDEX

© 2006 daab
cologne  london  new york

published and distributed worldwide by
daab gmbh
friesenstr. 50
d - 50670 köln

p +49-221-913 927 0
f +49-221-913 927 20

mail@daab-online.com
www.daab-online.com

publisher  ralf daab
rdaab@daab-online.com

creative director feyyaz
mail@feyyaz.com

editorial project by fusion publishing gmbh stuttgart . los angeles

editorial direction martin nicholas kunz
editorial coordination hanna martin, anne dörte schmidt
editor joachim fischer
introduction by frank bantle
english, french, spanish & italian translation ade team, stuttgart

layout anke scholz
imaging & pre-press jan hausberg

© 2006 fusion publishing, www.fusion-publishing.com

© frontcover photo paola de pietri
© introduction photos page 7 gaudenz danuser, page 8 jochen splett, page 9 jürgen schmidt

printed in slovenia
mkt print d.d., slovenia
www.mkt-print.com

isbn-10   3-937718-63-X
isbn-13   978-3-937718-63-7